Who are you?

Written and illustrated
by Emily Doan

This book belongs to;

_____

"Who are you?"
asked the sky.

"I am Lucy."
she replied.

"I don't like you"
blew the wind.

"...And I don't like to..."

Falllllllll

...Cried Lucy.
But then she
fell against the
wind...landing
somewhere
most strange...

"Where am I?"
asked Lucy...
"You are lost."
replied the Forest.

"It's rather lonely." said Lucy as she dawdled through the trees...

Only to find...

A
Mushroom
Kingdom?

"Who are you?"
asked Lucy.

"We are the villagers."
they replied.
"You are not one of us,
and you are different.
Who are you?"

"I am..."
Lucy couldn't speak as there was a loud noise throughout the kingdom.

A word was
yelled through the village, the
villagers were crying...

Giant...!

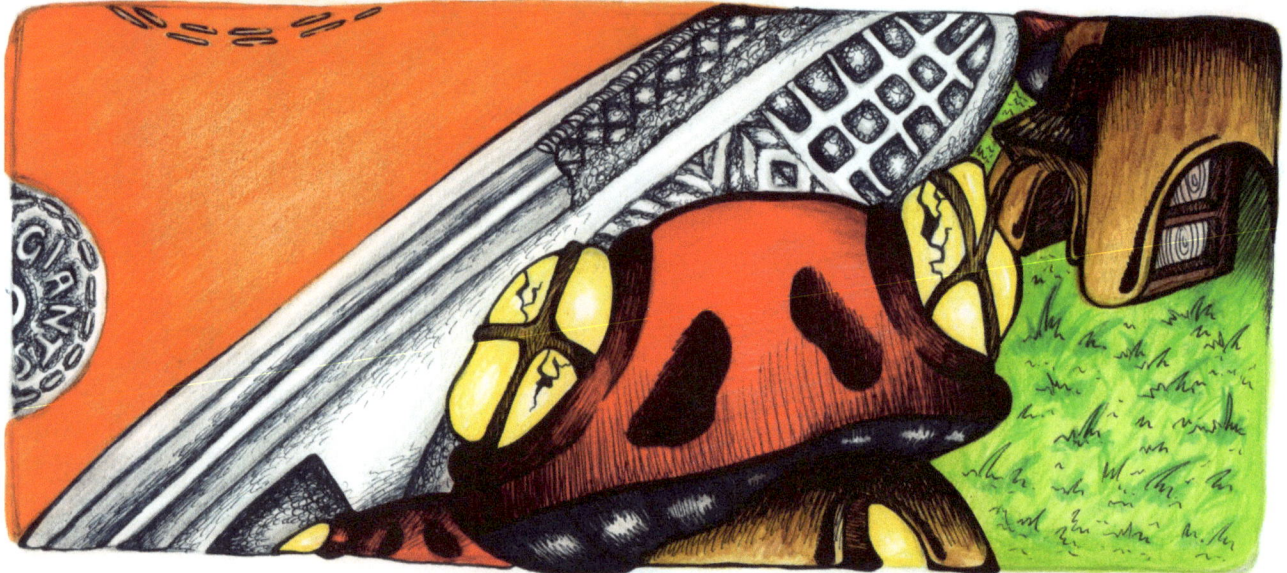

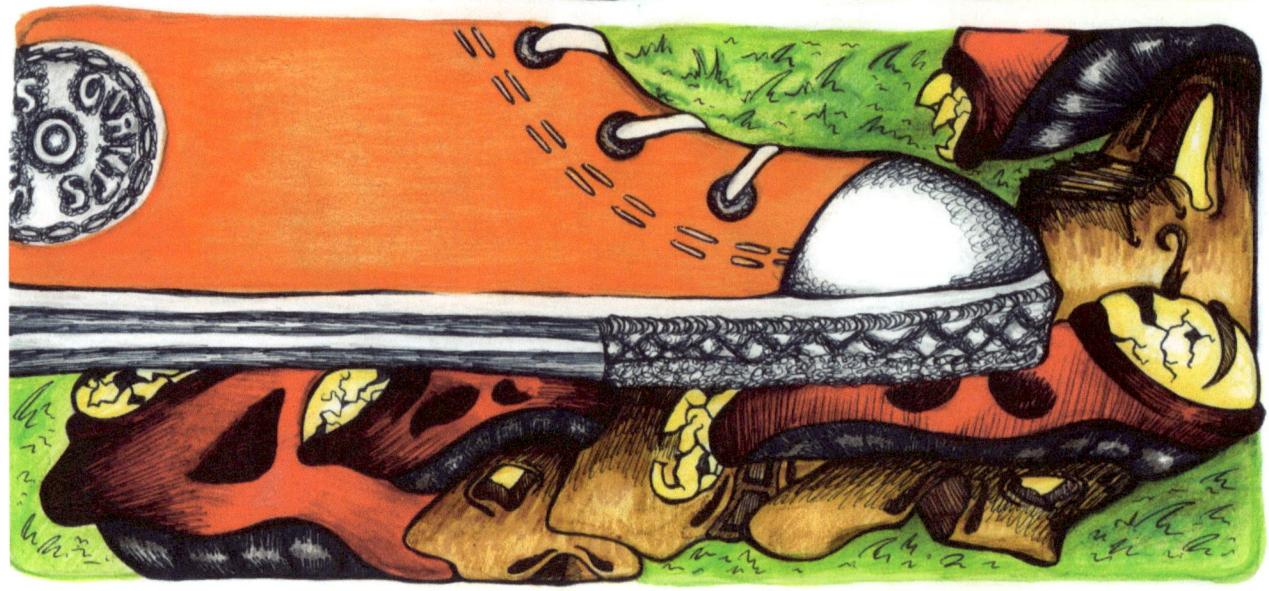

"Who? What? Where?" cried
Lucy, turning around seeing...
Nothing but a path of destruction.

"Please leave." muttered the Villagers.
"You are as strange as the Giant."
The simple villagers gave Lucy a
vehicle to send her
off on her way.

Confused, Lucy left, a little
sad, a little curious, thinking of the
unseen Giant. As her vehicle drove ahead
following the footsteps of the Giant,
she emerged into an enchanted garden.

"Who are you odd child?" spoke a voice from behind. "You do not belong here." "I am Lucy and..."

Lucy turned towards the voice, only to notice beautiful creatures. "What are you?" "We are the faerie folk." they replied with a snigger.

"And perhaps you know the whereabouts of the Giant's castle?"

"Follow us, and we will lead you there." Little did she know where she would go...

"A lake!"

Lucy realised
suddenly, turning
away from the
flowers. As she snapped
out of her
day dream, the faeries
pushed
her into the water.

"Curious..." thought Lucy,

,and it was very curious indeed.

"Who are you?"
called out
Lucy.
"I am a giant
boy." he
replied.
"I was
searching
for a friend,
I didn't see that
there were Villagers
below me... I am too tall, too
different and a bit
lonely.

Hearing this Lucy realised
that she felt the same,
small, different... but no
longer lonely. The boy, now
puzzled looked at Lucy
and questioned
"Who are you?"
asked the boy.

"I am your friend."
she replied.